John Scott Waring

Observations on the Present State of the East India Company

And on the Measures to be Pursued for Ensuring its Permanency, and Augmenting its Commerce

John Scott Waring

Observations on the Present State of the East India Company
And on the Measures to be Pursued for Ensuring its Permanency, and Augmenting its Commerce

ISBN/EAN: 9783337059378

Printed in Europe, USA, Canada, Australia, Japan

Cover: Foto ©ninafisch / pixelio.de

More available books at **www.hansebooks.com**

OBSERVATIONS

ON THE

PRESENT STATE

OF THE

EAST INDIA COMPANY;

AND ON THE

MEASURES TO BE PURSUED

FOR

Ensuring its PERMANENCY, and augmenting its COMMERCE.

LONDON,
Printed for J. NOURSE, Bookseller to His MAJESTY.
MDCCLXXI.

OBSERVATIONS

ON THE

PRESENT STATE

OF THE

EAST INDIA COMPANY'S AFFAIRS.

MY occupation and employment, for ſome years paſt, have given me many opportunities of enquiring into the ſtate of India, whereby I have obtained ſome knowledge of thoſe countries, that are more immediately connected with our poſſeſſions in thoſe parts; and having turned my thoughts towards the trade, as well as the government of our territories in that part of the world; I am able to give the public ſome information upon theſe intereſting ſubjects, which are growing every day more and more important to Great Britain.—My ſituation has preſerved me from all Indian connections; in which reſpect, I am more likely to be impartial than any of thoſe gentlemen, who have been concerned in the management

ment

ment of our affairs, either at home or abroad.—Nor have I ever meddled in the ſtocks, and, therefore, have no private intereſt in the riſe or fall of dividends.—I can anſwer for the facts that I have advanced; but my obſervations are ſubmitted to the public.—The reader will ſoon find that I have not been much accuſtomed to writing, and is not, therefore, to expect fine language, and well turned periods; but he may be aſſured, that the opinions are honeſt, and the facts are authentic, which, perhaps, may be ſufficient to recommend any eſſay upon a ſubject where the public wants information more than amuſement.

For theſe twelve or fourteen years paſt, a private body of merchants, belonging to a nation very far removed from the Mogul empire, have taken a principal part in the tranſactions of the great peninſula of India. A particular detail of the various circumſtances, which firſt led to, and have ſince produced, ſuch vaſt acquiſitions to the Eaſt India Company, is now of no conſequence; but it is of conſequence to know why the nation has profited ſo little from them. It is therefore the intention of theſe ſheets to point out thoſe errors which experience has diſcovered in the general conduct of our affairs, that the government may, before it is too late, endeavour to turn

the

the acquiſitions to that great account they are ſo capable of.

The Company's affairs, until about the year 1750, required little more than commercial talents; the produce of our own country was carried there, ſold, and returned in the manufactures of thoſe parts; and the little ſpots we poſſeſſed excited no jealouſies amongſt the neighbouring princes.

The French, under Duplex, firſt opened the way to acquiring territorial poſſeſſions in India; and why they did not reap thoſe advantages we have ſince done, and which they may be juſtly charged with having forced us into, on that coaſt, aroſe entirely from the miſconduct of Duplex, who, intoxicated by pride and vanity, did, through his obſtinacy, plunge his countrymen into various diſtreſſes, until they were quite undone. The ſucceſs, which at firſt attended his meaſures, was owing in a great degree to our inactivity and wretched parſimony. Mr. Barnet, who had foreſeen the ſtorm that was gathering, died unfortunately at the beginning of 1746, and Madraſs was taken the latter end of that year.

The leaders in the direction at that time, attentive only to the commercial plan, and prejudiced againſt more extenſive views, remained inactive until the French and Indian powers together had almoſt drove us into the ſea. We were rouſed at laſt by neceſſity; and, about the year 1751, the Company's affairs began to wear a better aſpect: lord Clive had made a ſtand againſt the enemy; and ſoon after general Laurence returned again from Europe to take upon him the chief command; his lordſhip acted under the general, and aſſiſted him in eſtabliſhing the reputation of the Britiſh arms.

About the year 1755, we were almoſt extirpated at Bengal, by the diſputes between Drake and Surajah Dowla, but were fortunately re-eſtabliſhed by lord Clive and admiral Watſon. Lord Clive went farther; he placed us on a footing all Europeans had been ſtrangers to before; for, by virtue of his treaties and conqueſts, we took the lead at the Suba's court. Soon after all this was ſettled, lord Clive returned to England, haſtened in ſome meaſure by a peremptory letter from the directors.

This increaſe of riches and power, joined to the intercourſe we had with the natives, both at Bengal and in the Carnatic, enabled us to obtain a more immediate, and a fuller knowledge of the country, its wealth and natural advantages, the number of its inhabitants, their manners, cuſtoms, and religions; and to preſerve our revenues, we found it neceſſary, that nothing material ſhould be done by the princes near us, without our approbation.

An

An extenſive commerce is the great and capital advantage which England ought to expect from theſe acquiſitions; and conſequently the politics of India ſhould be principally directed to this end; but though, perhaps, it might be wiſhed, that the original plan of trade, upon which the Company was firſt conſtituted, had ſtill continued upon that contracted bottom, and that they had not been from merchants erected into ſovereign princes; yet, as this great dominion is acquired, it muſt be maintained; for the politics, not only of Aſia, but even of Europe, are now ſo interwoven with the affairs of our commerce there, that it will be abſolutely impoſſible to return back to our former ſituation with any hopes of profit, or indeed of ſecurity: we muſt preſerve what we have acquired upon the principles of ſelf-defence.

Let us relinquiſh our poſſeſſions whenever we will, other Europeans are in readineſs to lay hold upon whatever we leave; or, if they could poſſibly be reſtored to the princes of the country, the memory of former conqueſts would naturally infuſe ſuch a reaſonable dread of future attacks into the minds of theſe princes, that they would never reſt till they had totally extirpated the Engliſh out of India; nor would treaties or engagements be of any avail with princes, who have no other principles of government but what ſpring from thoſe powerful paſſions, fear and hatred, and have no idea of national faith and honour.

It was not ambition that firſt tempted the Company to embark in theſe wars: neceſſity led the way; and conqueſt has now brought them to the choice either of dominion or expulſion. To ſay the truth, the natives and Europeans had, by degrees, obtained ſo much knowledge of each other, that, ſooner or later, this conflict muſt have happened, though it was haſtened by the unruly ambition of Duplex upon the Coromandel coaſt, and the miſconduct of Drake in Bengal. Self-preſervation firſt awakened us, and conqueſt gained us the great advantages we enjoy; force only can preſerve them; we muſt be all, or nothing; and ſurely it is better to die at once, than waſte away by inches; much loſs of men and treaſure might thereby be ſaved to the nation.

The great endeavour of all commercial ſtates, is to draw the productions of other countries to its own center; to work up the raw, and to re-export the manufactured goods; for wherever goods, though manufactured abroad, can be carried out again for ſale, ſo as to produce a final balance in favour of the ſtate, they are in a degree as me-

meritorious, in the eye of trade, as if they were manufactured at home: but, in a public light, the advantages that flow from a monopoly of carriage are far ſuperior to the dry profit of the merchant; to wit, the encreaſe of ſailors and ſhipping, and the employment of multitudes; all which add ſtrength as well as riches to the community. The act of navigation was founded upon this principle, by which this kingdom is become the greateſt maritime power that ever exiſted.

A fair opportunity now ſeems to offer, that may enable this kingdom, in a few years, to center in itſelf almoſt all the trade to the Eaſt Indies, and thereby to ſupply the reſt of Europe from the mart of London. To effect ſo great an undertaking, a revenue muſt be allotted, ſufficient to maintain a ſtrong ſquadron in India always ready to fit out, and three ſeparate armies, one on the eaſt and one on the weſt coaſt of the peninſula, and one at Bengal. It is by ſuch ſteps only, that the conqueſts can become of any laſting or ſolid advantage; and that all this may be effected, I ſhall endeavour to ſhew: happy, if any of my hints may excite ſome abler head to digeſt, and bring them to perfection.

Lord Clive, when he returned home in February, 1760, left Mr. Holwel in the chair

chair at Bengal, who was superseded from Madrass, in August following, by Mr. Vansittart, a gentleman of a fair and amiable character, but unacquainted with that settlement. Immediately on his arrival, the conduct of Meer Jaffier was placed in such a light, as induced him, by a fatal revolution, to place Cossim Cawn on the throne. The stain of wanton tyranny this action left behind it, will long remain upon the minds of the natives: the whole of this blameable transaction, together with the many melancholy consequences, are too well known to need repeating: matters soon came to a crisis; one constant scene of anarchy and dissension prevailed from Cossim's ascending the throne to his flight: he fled at last, and carried with him *a vast sum in specie.*

The principal reason given to the public for deposing Meer Jaffier, was the wretched state of his finances; but this arose from the misconduct and treachery of his ministers. That there was no real want of specie in the country, is manifest from the large sums which Cossim was enabled to collect, with such expedition, almost immediately after his advancement: and with how much ease might the Company have reformed his government, by a change of his miniſters, if they had pleaſed, without any diſturbance or commotion.

I am clearly of opinion it was as eaſy to reſtrain Meer Jaffier as to depoſe him; and the country would not, in that caſe, (to ſay nothing of the other miſchiefs occaſioned by that revolution) have been drained of that immenſe ſum which Coſſim carried off with him upon his expulſion: yet the country was not totally exhauſted even by this drain, witneſs the ſums that have been ſent out, ſince his flight, to Madraſs, Bombay, and China.

In the year 1764, Meer Jaffier was replaced in the ſubaſhip; conteſts, and the purſuit of private gain, continued abroad, and party ran high at home. It was at this time lord Clive again ſtood forth to take upon him the command at Bengal. He ſet off in May, 1764, and did not reach Calcutta until April, 1765. He found Meer Jaffier dead, when he arrived; he gave that Nabob's ſon the outward pageantry of Suba, but the power and the revenues he took charge of for the company; he allotted out of them a certain ſtipend for the nominal Suba, and for the Mogul, the tribute theſe provinces uſed to remit to Delhi, when the empire was properly ſettled; the remainder of the revenues was brought into the treaſury of Calcutta.

The ſubaſhip of Bengal takes in a large extent of country, the greateſt part of which is under the Suba's immediate direction; the remainder is under the management of Nabobs, Rajahs, or Polygars, who are to pay certain annual tributes to the Suba, and ſome of them are likewiſe to bring into the field a certain number of troops whenever they are required, the management of the lands within their reſpective governments being left entirely to themſelves to farm and to collect. The diſtracted ſtate the empire had long been in, had led the Suba to neglect paying the tribute due to the throne of Delhi; and the enfeebled ſtate of Shaw Allum made him incapable of enforcing his right; but ſince we have had poſſeſſion, that uſual tribute has been regularly paid.

The whole revenue above mentioned, including the tribute payable to the Great Mogul, amounts to the ſum of near three millions four hundred thouſand pounds; to which may be added the duties collected on the foreign trade at the port of Calcutta, about twenty thouſand pounds. Beſides all this, the Company are in the receipts of a conſiderable ſum for the duties upon ſalt, beetel, and tobacco. This brought in, while the monopoly of thoſe articles took place, about one hundred and twenty thou-

ſand

sand pounds a year, but, since that was abolished, is reduced to one hundred thousand pounds, or under. The whole of this revenue may be fairly set at three millions five hundred thousand pounds, out of which the * tribute to the Mogul, the allotment to the Nabob, the expence of collecting the revenue, and the civil and military charges of government at Bengal, altogether amount to about two millions, though I am pretty sure it is not quite so much, and consequently there ought to remain the sum of one million five hundred thousand pounds, neat income, in the hands of the Company, to be applied for the purchase of the home investments, or for any emergencies that might accidentally arise. The province of Orixa, which properly belongs to the Suba of Bengal, is now in the hands of Morattahs: it yields a revenue of about one hundred and thirty thousand pounds. This province might be easily recovered; and it is well defended by hills that bound it to the S. W.

	£.
* The tribute to the Mogul, —— ——	330,000
The Nabob, for his court, 18 lacks, charge of collecting the revenue, 35 lacks,	670,000
The civil and military expences, with the amount of stores of different kinds, about —— —— ——	1,000,000
	2,000,000

The preſent eſtabliſhment of the forces at Bengal is fixed at three thouſand Europeans, and near * twenty thouſand Seipoys or country infantry; all of whom are regularly diſciplined, and formed into battalions, and are commanded by European officers; this force is reckoned ſufficient to defend the provinces againſt all invaſions.

† The prince is the lord proprietor of the lands, his will is under no controul; nevertheleſs, the mode of farming out the lands continues amongſt the Morattahs, and all the Gentoos, in much the ſame ſtate it was in before the Moors got poſſeſſion of the empire.

The lands are under the direction either of officers ſuperintending for the Mogul, or princes who, collecting for themſelves, pay annual tributes to the empire; and no lands are exempted from paying a proportion to the crown, but thoſe belonging to pagodas, moſques, or enjoying ſome other privileges. Theſe lands amongſt the Morattahs, are granted to the occupiers for a term of years, or for life, which laſt method moſtly prevails; and provided

* This number does not include the Seipoys employed by the revenue officers.

† Princes holding large tracts of country, have other princes under them, in like manner as they hold under the Mogul.

no charge lays againſt them for embezzlement, or neglect of tillage, there is ſcarcely an inſtance of the lands being taken from the families of the firſt occupiers. The ſame maxims prevail with reſpect to the Rajahs and great officers, who were always permitted to hold by deſcent, and were ſcarce ever diſplaced, except for miſgovernment or rebellion. * The lands pay according to their produce; this is taken by collectors for the prince, who calling in men converſant in huſbandry, do, by their judgment, ſet the value of the prince's ſhare while the crop is on the ground; the value, ſo ſettled, is what the occupier is to pay, and this is tranſmitted, by the ſeveral collectors, to the treaſurer or Duan, who is commonly the firſt miniſter of the prince. The grain uſually pays one half of its produce, cocoa-nut and beetel-nut trees two-thirds, fruit trees, and thoſe converted into wood and timber one-third; buffaloes pay one rupee each (or half-a-crown), draft oxen not ſo much, a-year; and ſo every other article in proportion, that is produced by, or nouriſhed from the earth.

The prince's revenue is neat and clear of all deduction, except the fees to the

* Moſt of the lands in the ſouthern parts of the empire yield double crops.

Duan,

Duan, for himſelf and his collectors, which are fixed, and publicly known; what remains over and above the produce due to the prince, belongs to the occupier of the lands; and this is found, by experience, when he is permitted to enjoy it, to be an ample reward to him for his labour and expence.

This mode of collection has an appearance of the ſtricteſt juſtice, and is founded on principles of equity, but is obviouſly liable to be corrupted in practice, becauſe it leaves a large field for knavery and extortion. The occupier of the land is in no wiſe on an equal footing with the collector; and the inferior claſſes of men are kept in ſuch vaſt ſubordination, in thoſe oppreſſive governments, that fear prevents their complaints; the juſteſt are often conſtrued into murmurs and diſcontents, and puniſhed, probably, with the ſevereſt chaſtiſements; for what can thoſe poor wretches do, or what redreſs can they hope to find, when their judges have, perhaps, ſhared the plunder with thoſe very * oppreſſors they come to complain againſt.

* Seeking redreſs from the Zemindars or Patels, in their judicial capacity, who are in league with, or act under the farmers and collectors in gathering in the revenues.

The

The Moors, in the countries under their immediate government, have made ſome alteration in the mode of collecting the revenue, but not at all calculated to ſecure the occupier of the land from oppreſſion. The princes, to be at the greater certainty, portioned out the lands in their ſeveral provinces, into conſiderable diviſions, which were ſeverally farmed, or let on leaſe for the amount of the government's ſhare to the beſt bidder, which ſhare compriſed in it alſo the avowed fees for the officers of the revenue; this ſum the farmer of the revenue, for each diviſion or portion of lands, paid into the Suba or prince's treaſury he belonged to.

Whatever remained, after this ſhare ſo paid in, ought to have been the occupier's reward for his labour and expence. This is the cuſtom of the country, and the occupier would be happy, if the farmer of the revenue executed his office with any degree of equitable mercy; but the power of ſqueezing, which the farmer is intruſted with, for the purpoſe of collecting the lawful revenue, renders him ſo abſolute, that he extorts almoſt what he pleaſes from the poor occupier. Every man who aims at this employment, muſt pave the way to his appointment, by great preſents to the Nabob or his treaſurer, which muſt be often repeated, if he means to continue in his office. He that makes the largeſt preſent, is ſure to be preferred among the bidders; for, indeed, no perſon dares to bid againſt the man who is known to be favoured by the Duan. Theſe preſents to the great men, as well as the farmer's own profit, muſt be paid out of the occupier's reſidue; and thus, as extortion knows not where to ſtop, the miſerable occupier is at laſt driven from his land—the revenue falls ſhort, and the poor wretch, who is beggared by the avarice of his ſuperiors, is frequently made the victim of the deficiency, as if it was owing to his want of induſtry, and not to the rapacity of the farmers, and the great miniſters of the prince.

This being the nature, and theſe the methods of collecting the revenue, the poor ſubject has in all times been oppreſſed by Duans, farmers, and collectors.—Theſe ways to wealth are eaſy and expeditious; to which, if you add the practice of making preſents (which is an eſtabliſhed cuſtom in India) the great men and miniſters grow rich in an inſtant; but as theſe were always in danger of being plundered again by their ſovereign, the dread, together with the fear of puniſhment, taught ſome to be more moderate; and thoſe who were directed, either by prudence or juſtice, treated the natives with ſome degree of gentleneſs; and ſo the country continued in a tolerable ſtate of proſperity, even under the rapacity of abſolute government. When this revenue came under the management of the Company, lord Clive continued the ſame mode of collecting, and the nominal Duan, farmers, and collectors were ſtill Moors or natives, and they ſtill bore the title of miniſters and ſervants to the nominal Nabob; but were under the inſpection and controul of the Board.

The treaſurer or Duan, appointed by lord Clive, was Mahomed Reza Caun; it was left to him to nominate, and to preſide over the ſeveral collectors and farmers of the revenue; and as they brought in the money, he delivered it to a gentleman, a member of the Board of Calcutta, who tranſmitted the amount to the Company's treaſury. This gentleman was fixed at the Durbar, to ſuperintend Mahomed Reza Caun, and to tranſact the buſineſs of Cozambazar, where the ſilk inveſtments are moſtly made; and to be watchful, at the ſame time, of any intrigues carried on amongſt the great officers about the perſon of the nominal Suba.

Gentlemen were likewiſe fixed in the country, to ſuperintend the revenues of thoſe lands firſt ceded to us, and which are more particularly called the Company's Lands. The ſame mode of collecting was ſtill continued, with this difference only, that the farmers of the revenue were appointed from year to year, whereas they had generally been for a term of years: this was intended to prevent making improper bargains, but it only drove the farmers to the neceſſity of annually repeating their preſents to Mahomed Raza Caun, who, with the Durbar reſident, directed the ſeveral portions of the lands to be publicly put up, and granted to the beſt bidder; the management and intrigues of the officers ſtruck them down always to him, who privately made the largeſt preſent to the Duan, nor could the European gentlemen prevent it; ſo that the occupier of the lands has not only to raiſe the proportion due to the crown, but to furniſh as much more as is neceſſary for the emolument, as well as the reimburſement, of the farmer, who muſt extort for the Duan, as well as for themſelves. If the occupiers complained of the oppreſſion, and the European gentlemen interfered, they were deterred by the aſſurances of the collectors, that their complaints were unreaſonable, and that it would be impoſſible for them to collect the revenues, if lenity

was

was exercised; as it was a general maxim with them to murmur, and, if possible, to evade their rent.—The occupier incapable, from this cruel treatment, of supporting his family and the expence of tillage, is obliged either to till the lands in a very negligent manner, or to relinquish them entirely, and seek subsistence elsewhere.

Mahomed Raza Caun, his officers, and the farmers, who at this time manage the revenue, center with themselves, not only the extortion just mentioned, but besides all this, those thirty-five lack, which are taken from the revenue for the charge of collecting, are intrusted in the disposal of Mahomed Raza Caun: he is very rich, and would have been much richer, but for his great liberality to his friends.

These are the true causes of the instability of this revenue, which must always fall short to the Company, so long as the occupiers are thus drained by a tribe of Duans and officers of the revenue.——This practice is, in truth, an embezzlement of the revenue itself; for there is little or no difference between plundering the treasury, after the money is collected, and taking from the fund out of which it is to arise; the deficiency to the public is the same in both cases.

But besides these practices, which had always prevailed in this country to some degree, our countrymen struck out a new method of acquiring immense sums by trade, as they call it, and by drawing to themselves the most destructive monopoly, that ever was invented.——For the great power and influence we acquired throughout the provinces belonging to Bengal, opened a new scene of traffic with the interior parts of the country, which our former weakness had always rendered us incapable of undertaking. This trade consisted mostly in salt, beetel, and tobacco; the two last are, as much as the first, reckoned by the Indians amongst the necessaries of life.——This trade was begun by us under Meer Jaffier; all ranks of men run into it, tempted by the great profits these articles always yielded, which must be the case when goods are carried to great distances, are very bulky, and invest but little money.—And these advantages were greatly increased to the European gentlemen, as they evaded the heavy customs, and at last demanded the privilege of trading free from every restraint; very considerable fortunes were made by this trade.

Necessity did for some time oblige the Subas to yield to this unjustifiable proceeding;

ing; but at laſt Coſſim, thinking himſelf ſecurely ſeated on the throne, loudly exclaimed againſt theſe irregularities, and remonſtrated to Mr. Vanſittart, that very fatal conſequences, highly injurious to the ſtate, would ariſe, if a proper reſtraint was not laid on thoſe gentlemen who puſhed on this trade in ſo unprecedented a manner. Coſſim complained that theſe licentious meaſures deprived him of a conſiderable part of his revenue; that his own ſubjects, who had uſually paid twenty-five *per cent.* on thoſe articles, could no longer trade upon an equal footing; that the Engliſh gentlemen, who had hitherto only paid two and a half *per cent.* now refuſed paying any duty at all.—It muſt be remembered, Mr. Vanſittart endeavoured to bring this under a proper regulation, for the benefit of all parties, by fixing it at nine per cent. but unfortunately he was over-ruled.——The vaſt profits this trade yielded, drew every body into it.——Free merchants and mariners crouded without number to India; and embarking with the Company's ſervants, who remained fixed always to one ſpot, undertook the management of it, and ſhared the profits——the whole paſſing under the duſtucks, or privileges of the Company's ſervants. Such of the natives as were mercantile ſervants to the Englifh gentlemen, gained very confiderably, and paid great fums of money for the privileges they obtained through their mafters; whilft the real merchant of the country, labouring under the tax of heavy duties, and oppreffed by the brokers and managers for the Europeans, were forced to give up a trade, they could no longer carry on upon an equal footing.

When lord Clive arrived the fecond time, and took the revenues from the Suba, his lordfhip, together with his council, formed the extenfive trade carried on throughout the provinces for falt, beetel, and tobacco, into a monopoly, under the management of a company, equally fhutting out both natives and foreigners.

To make room for this monopoly, the Board called down all the Europeans difperfed about the provinces, and forbid any going up, without their previous licence. This feemed neceffary, and calculated to anfwer a wife purpofe; for, when his lordfhip arrived, the unfettled ftate of the government had led numbers to take advantage of it; who, fpreading themfelves throughout the provinces, were eagerly purfuing trade where-ever they went.

But unfortunately the means adopted for correcting this abuse, only introduced a worse; for the * monopoly that followed, became

* I cannot believe the gentlemen who planed the monopoly, foresaw the extent of its pernicious consequences. The plan was, first, an exclusive company to carry on the trade in salt, beetel, and tobacco, consisting of all who may be deemed justly entitled to a share; a proper fund to be raised for its support by loan at interest. All salt, beetel, and tobacco produced in, or imported into Bengal, to be purchased by the society, and all other persons excluded. The nabob to be applied to, to issue such prohibition throughout the districts, where those articles are manufactured or produced. The articles to be purchased on the most moderate terms by contract.——The above articles, purchased by the society, to be transported to certain places, and there disposed of by their agents. The purchasers to have liberty of again transporting them whither they please.—The East India Company to be considered as proprietors, or receive an annual duty on it, as may appear most to their interest, when considered with their other interests and demands on this presidency.——The Nabob to be considered as may be judged most proper, either as a proprietor, or by an annual allowance, to be computed on inspecting a statement of his duties on salt in former years.—It being determined in what manner the Company and Nabob shall be considered, the remainder to be divided amongst the Company's servants, according to their different classes.——A committee of trade to be appointed to carry this plan into execution.—The Company having obtained the grant of the Duanne, since the last consultation, the article relative to the Nabob was declared of non-effect.—The Company, therefore, to be considered as superiors, and not to share with the society, but to receive the following duties, 35 per cent. on salt, 10 ditto on beetel-nut, 25 ditto on tobacco.

became ten times more pernicious than the open trade had been; for now the provinces were slowly supplied with the necessaries of life, and the prices were greatly increased.

The salt brought from foreign markets, or made in the most distant parts of the provinces, could only be sold to the agents of this select company; all the beetel-nut and tobacco was sold in like manner. Every person trading in any of these articles, was obliged to purchase their entire stock from the company. This restraint had so bad an effect, that the prices to the consumer were enormously enhanced. To instance in the article of salt only, the same quantity that was sold, before this monopoly, and well sold, for eighty rupees, sold after the combination at the encreased price of two hundred.——The method of carrying on this trade was curious. The Company at home were entitled to receive a duty of thirty-five per cent. upon this commodity *ad valorem*; the company abroad (for so I must have leave to call the monopolists) set the price at the salt-pans upon the manufacture as low as they thought fit, and paid the duty upon the price so settled. Thus having obtained the property, they sold the same at their own advanced price to others, who were

were to retail it in the country. By this management ſalt, an article ſo univerſally neceſſary, and which before the duty was paid, was the cheapeſt drug in India, became immediately after that payment the deareſt.

The inevitable conſequence of ſuch a proceeding, is that the manufactures muſt be enhanced to repay the conſumer, and that the Company's intereſt muſt be ſacrificed for the advantage of a few individuals, who would, by theſe means, divide a premium amongſt themſelves of one hundred per cent. beyond a reaſonable profit, on the neceſſaries of life; which, from the amazing conſumption on each of thoſe articles, muſt amount to a very large ſum of money.

Whilſt the Europeans, before this monopoly, traded on better terms than the natives, by evading the duties, it was the revenue only that ſuffered, and the natives were excluded, by being under-ſold. For if in that caſe the European merchant had raiſed his price upon the conſumer beyond its value, together with the amount of the duty; the natives would have reſumed the trade, by which means the price of thoſe articles could never be advanced to a pitch that would raiſe the manufactures.—Whereas the monopoly had

 the

the moſt pernicious, ruinous effect; it was calculated to injure the occupier of the land, to affect the ſecurity of the revenue, and to enhance the prices of all the goods made throughout the provinces.

It is eaſy to judge how all the manufactures muſt riſe, when the neceſſaries of life became ſo dear! to ſay nothing of the deſertion of the people, many chuſing to leave a country, where the wages of labour fell ſo ſhort of the expence of ſubſiſtence.

Here, however, the directors muſt be acquitted, for they never approved of it; and, in leſs than two years from its eſtabliſhment, ordered it to be diſſolved, and renewed ſome former acts, totally forbidding the Engliſh to trade in any of theſe articles. Here the affair ended; but as no proper meaſures were taken to encourage the freedom of this trade, amongſt the real merchants of the country, though the monopoly is at home aboliſhed, the Europeans may, to this hour, have a principal ſhare in the trade, through the means of their black agents, if they chuſe it, and can at any time throw difficulties in the merchant's way, when he attempts to trade for himſelf.——While the ſervants abroad were ruining their maſters, by theſe pernicious practices, the directors were diſ-

treſſing

treſſing the Company by injudicious meaſures at home; for when this great ſtream of riches flowed into our treaſury, they thought themſelves in poſſeſſion of an inexhauſtible ſource of wealth——at leaſt their conduct gave room for the ſuppoſition; for money was laviſhly ſent away in ſpecie every year to * Bombay, Madraſs, and China, until the ſource was almoſt dried up.—This the Company could not have afforded, if the country could have borne it; for after near two millions are deducted for the neceſſary diſburſements of the ſettlement, and ſeven or eight hundred thouſand pounds are appropriated for the home inveſtments, the remainder will be found very inadequate to ſupply China, Bombay, and Madraſs, together with the expences of the fortifications, far from being completed, though continually raiſing, together with a neceſſary ſurplus, which ſhould be always laid by to anſwer the deficiency of bad years. The greateſt part of this money is gone for ever; and there is a loſs of ſix or eight per cent. upon the caſh carried to China, between the ſter-

* Bombay took away five or ſix † lacks every year.—Madraſs and China in four or five years, took away near a million and a half.

† A lack of rupees is 100,000 rupees, or about 12,500 l. a crore is 100 lack.

ling currency at Bengal and the value at Canton.

Theſe conſiderations, together wlth the injury ſuſtained by the country from the loſs of that wealth carried away by Coſſim, which will never come back, ſhould naturally have ſuggeſted ſome mode how to ſupply the provinces with ſpecie. Inſtead of that, the drains continued, and the ſcarcity was increaſed. The great increaſe of trade that naturally followed the great increaſe of our riches and power, required a quick circulation, and a large increaſe of money, to anſwer the additional demands, which will always riſe, in proportion as trade and manufactures are extended. The want of ſpecie will produce a ſtagnation of trade, eſpecially in a country where no faith reſts on paper credit. Drains and oppreſſions like theſe no country can bear.

The natives can have no inducements to bring forth thoſe treaſures fear led them to hide whilſt under their own Subas, if they are equally torn from them under us, and the means of ſubſiſtence rendered dearer. Thus, whilſt the gentlemen at home were ſo loudly exclaiming againſt the conduct of their ſervants abroad, inſtead of ſearching the diſeaſe to the bottom, the better to apply the remedy, they were purſuing meaſures equally deſtructive to the Company's intereſt

eſt, by ſending money out of the country never to return: nay, at one time, as I have been credibly informed, it was a matter of debate, whether ſome of it ſhould not be brought to Europe; but an exhauſted treaſury ſoon determined that point. How merchants could ever think of committing ſo groſs an error is aſtoniſhing! It was the like falſe policy that made the directors ſtop the remittance through their caſh from Bengal and elſewhere, in order to prevent an increaſe of the demands upon them in England. On this refuſal, the private fortunes, to a very large amount, went home through foreign bills; and, by this means, both French and Dutch went to market upon the ſame terms with the Company; and when the revenues fell off, or came in but ſlowly, on better terms, by being before us in their advancements for goods, at the aurongs, or markets, where they are manufactured.

If the Company had received the private fortunes into the ſeveral treaſuries in India, it would doubtleſs have protracted the payment of the ſimple contract-debts, and the reduction of any of the bond-debts; but then thoſe debts would have been only laying at an intereſt of either three, four, or five per cent. whilſt their money abroad would have been gaining an intereſt of eight or nine per cent.: beſides

besides, another advantage would have resulted from it; foreigners must either have brought silver to India, or have come to the mart of London.

As I have taken notice of the Company's debts, I cannot help lamenting, that the parliament should have been induced to join with the Company in sharing between them eight hundred thousand pounds a year, before any of these debts were discharged, or any funds securely established for their payment; because it looks rather too much like a bargain, both parties giving each other a consideration for dividing the money that should have gone to the creditors. It would have been more for the interest of the Company, and the public too, to have restrained the dividend altogether till the debts had been discharged.

But to return; I doubt not, but the natives will endeavour to * hide all the money they can from the various oppressions they groan under, whilst they see it passing so fast out of the country, and so thoroughly experience the distress arising to the country in general from such a drain.

All that supply we used to bring annually into Bengal, is entirely stopt; and our ill-

* Amongst the Gentoos, it is a general maxim, to hide one third, to invest a third in jewels, and keep the other for use and trade.

judged

judged conduct has saved foreigners the trouble of carrying specie thither. Where are the sums required for the exigencies of trade to be found, for the farmer to pay his rent with, for the merchant and manufacturer to carry on trade through all its various branches, and to answer all the great disbursements the company have continually to make throughout that extensive settlement?

When we consider the advantages that formerly used to arise, in a course of years, to the gentlemen residing at Calcutta, and the subordinate factories, from a trade fettered by the natives with various embarrassments, and circumscribed as to articles; when we reflect how much the trade has been extended in all the former articles, and none of the valuable ones now exempted; when we reflect, that the chiefs of Patna and Decca are under no controul from the natives; when we recollect the great profits arising to the districts of Chittagon and Luckapore from a most extensive trade in beetel-nut and tobacco; when we consider the advantages the residents at Midnapore, at Birdwan, and Malda enjoy; and when we reflect, that the natives, unless through our assistance, or that of our mercantile servants, trade to infinite disadvantage,

vantage, and that the whole will naturally center where the ſeveral chiefs and principals above enumerated think proper; when we review the number of free merchants, who, until the year 1766, ranged uncontrouled about the inland parts, many of whom have acquired genteel fortunes; we ſhall be able to account for ſome part of that wealth, which has, of late years, been the ſubject of ſo much diſcourſe.

When we take a review of the great power given to the Durbar reſident, to ſuperintend the conduct of the Duan; and that the ſilk inveſtments center in the chief of Caſſambazar; that the unfortunate Shaw Allum, the Duan, and all the different princes, were over-awed by the power of the governor, and were ſurrounded by generals, who were ready to unſheath the ſword upon the leaſt diſturbance; when we add to theſe accounts the contracts for the different branches of fortifications and other public buildings, for the victualling armies, and for the ſupply of the different exigencies of ſo great a ſtate; we cannot long be at a loſs to account for all thoſe various fortunes, from twenty thouſand up to two hundred thouſand pounds, brought home within theſe fourteen years paſt, the greateſt part of which have been acquired within ſhort ſpaces of time.

It

It cannot be imagined, men will ſerve through ſuch various hazards as they are expoſed to in India, and at ſuch a diſtance from their native country, without the proſpect of ſome conſiderable reward, eſpecially ſurrounded as they are on every ſide with wealth. This no reaſonable or prudent man can expect. Fortunes ſhould by all means be attainable; but neither ſo rapidly, nor with ſo much eaſe, as of late years: they ſhould be acquired by fair and open traffic, by the legal ample emoluments to be annexed to the higher offices, and to great truſts; not by the ſervile mode of preſents, and by vile monopolies.

In taking a review of the Company's great acquiſitions at Bengal, we find an army, with the revenue to ſupport it, without any aſſiſtance from England; we have ſeen ſucceſs, for many years paſt, attend it wherever it went forth; and we know that force to be ſufficient for the defence of our poſſeſſions, and ſuch as no European powers can ſtand againſt: we find the Nabob of Oude, our moſt dangerous enemy about Bengal, brought within bounds; and the king freed from his fetters.

The confuſion and diſtreſs the country had been expoſed to required care and indulgence to recover it: inſtead of that, the ſame arbitrary modes have prevailed; luxury and indolence have increaſed to an aſtoniſhing height, and pervaded every rank of men; the crown-rents have been collected with the ſame rapacity as they were under the Subas; the ſame extortion has prevailed, and the ſame cruelties were committed, that had been practiſed under the former deſpotiſm; great complaints have aroſe of the difficulty of collecting, and clamours of the ſcarcity of money; but, nevertheleſs, individuals made large and rapid fortunes; the money brought into the treaſury has been locked up, or was elſe ſent out of the country; the neceſſaries of life have been too much engroſſed; foreigners have had the uſe of the private property; and every meaſure has been directly oppoſite to the real intereſt of the country.

All our diſtreſſes are compriſed within thoſe three heads: the injudicious mode of collecting the revenues; enhancing the prices on the neceſſaries of life; and ſending away the money, never to return.

In India, as in all other deſpotic governments, mankind are bridled only by fear: this leads men to hide or diſſipate their money as faſt as they acquire it; both are equally injurious to trade. Many of the natives of India had gained ſome general knowledge of the principles of our conſtitution: they knew, that it adopted an inherent right in every individual to whatever he poſſeſſed, either from ſucceſſion or induſtry; and that certain fixed and immutable laws were the guardians and ſecurity of that right, and the barrier againſt the caprice and paſſions of thoſe who governed. From this conſideration, I know, the natives, eſpecially the induſtrious part, were very deſirous of our influence prevailing; becauſe, from their ideas of our government, they depended on accumulating wealth with ſafety. But, alas, how greatly have they been deceived!

The firſt ſtep that ought to have been taken, was to have ſecured to the inhabitants the neceſſaries of life, over all the provinces, on the moſt beneficial terms, by leaving them open to all the natives, under every poſſible encouragement; carefully guarding againſt every private embarraſſment that might be thrown in their way, and fixing the duties in the moſt equitable and reaſonable manner; they would then have yielded the Company a very handſome revenue, and the inhabitants would have bought them at an eaſier rate, than they ever did before. The crown-rents, ariſing from the lands, ought to have been collected with care and tenderneſs; every aſſiſtance ſhould have been given the occupiers; every man's quota, according to the goodneſs and quantity of his ground, declared in the moſt public manner; and every meaſure carefully taken, to prevent indolence and inattention on the part of the Europeans, and rapacity on that of the Indian collectors. That this was ever properly done, I deny.

The real dues of the crown were eaſily obtained from the public books. If the occupier of the land had once been taught, that, upon paying his proper quota, the remainder ſhould have been ſecure from the hand of any invader whatever, the farmers of the revenues would have been needleſs, the number of collectors might have been reduced, and the reſt reſtrained from all thoſe oppreſſions, which their power tempted them to inflict, from the ſecurity they enjoyed, by keeping the occupiers poor, and bribing thoſe above them. If the occupier had been releaſed from every burden but what he owed his prince, the remainder would have been ſo full a reward, that he would have been very careful not to have riſked the loſs of his lands by evading his rent. Mankind are ſeldom wanting in a knowledge of their real intereſt; and whenever it is blended with our own, we may be ſatisfied our own will never be neglected. Inſtead of ſending a ſingle rupee out of the provinces, care ſhould be taken to encourage the Gulph and Manilla trades, the only

erremaining ſources for ſpecie, when the Company ceaſed to ſend ſilver from Europe: neither of theſe were ever thought of, as worthy public conſideration. I dare maintain, that had the revenues been collected with a proper attention to the laſting intereſt of the country; if every poſſible encouragement had been given to the trade of ſalt, beetel, and tobacco; if no ſilver had been ſent out of the country, but circulated for the benefit of the manufactures and tillage; we ſhould have been much nearer thoſe great national advantages ſo reaſonably expected, and at firſt ſo laviſhly promiſed.

The meaſures hitherto purſued have only tended to thin the country, by driving the natives, through diſtreſs, to ſeek ſubſiſtence elſewhere; to reduce the revenues; to encreaſe the price of the manufactures; and to make us feared, hated, and deſpiſed: the two laſt will remain, the firſt will vaniſh as our internal ſtrength decays; and which, I am afraid, it is doing very faſt.

PART

PART II.

Considerations on the State of the Coromandel and Malabar Coasts.

THE wars carried on in the Carnatic, for the ſpace of ten or eleven years, from 1751 to 1762, will ever reflect honour on the conductors in behalf of Great Britain. The Carnatic was, by their means, reſtored to peace, plenty, and commerce. The Nabob, rid of all his enemies, ſaw himſelf in the full poſſeſſion of one of the fineſt countries in the peninſula; and in condition ſpeedily to reimburſe the Company for all the expences of the war and the riſk they had run together. Our troops, that guarded his frontiers and the paſſes into the Carnatic, not only placed him in ſecurity from his natural enemies, the Nizam and Hyder Ally, but kept him likewiſe in a proper ſtate of dependence upon the Company.

In this ſituation lord Pigot left the Carnatic in 1763, and retired from the government, after having, for the ſpace of nine years,

years, ſtruggled with, and ſurmounted dangers and diſtreſſes, that had almoſt overwhelmed the ſettlement. His lordſhip's conduct will always do honour to his character. The Carnatic reaches from Maſulapatnam down to Tanjour, taking in an extent of near three hundred miles along the coaſt, and no where more than about ninety or one hundred miles in breadth: it is bounded to the northward by the Nizam's dominions, to ſome part of which it is open; to the weſtward it is ſeparated from the Decan and Miſour countries by one continued ridge of mountains, over which are ſome few paſſes or * gotts, difficult to force; to the ſouth it joins Madura and the Tanjour country, and on this ſide can only be entered by the plains of Trichanopoly. This whole country is very fertile, and abounds with manufactures, on which account it is the moſt beneficial province for our trade, as it affords a very large quantity of white cloths, great part of which, after they are ſtained in England, are exported to a very conſiderable amount. Our own proper ſettlement conſiſts in a ſmall tract of country about Madraſs, and a further ceſſion at Maſulapatnam and Niſampatnam; theſe,

* Two or three of theſe defiles are in the poſſeſſion of Hyder Ally, reſtored to him by the laſt treaty.

together with the five northern circars or provinces, extending from a little above Maſulapatnam up to Orixa, ought to yield the Company, in a ſettled flouriſhing ſtate, a revenue of near ſeven hundred thouſand pounds a year. Our expence, on that coaſt, amounts annually to about two hundred and fifty thouſand pounds; ſo that a conſiderable ſurplus ought to lay in the treaſury of Madraſs, for trade and other demands. The military eſtabliſhment of Fort St. George conſiſts of three thouſand Europeans, and about fourteen thouſand black infantry, diſciplined on the ſame plan as thoſe at Bengal. Great part of the troops being employed for the defence of the Carnatic, they are paid by the * Nabob, whoſe frontiers are garriſoned every way by our troops. Nizam Ally ſtiles himſelf Suba of the Decan, but retains none of that power his father, Nizam Al-Muluch, enjoyed. The dominions he left his poſterity reached almoſt from ſea to ſea; but, ſince the ceſſion of the five northern circars to us, in 1766, they are now wholly inland, and reduced every way. Theſe five circars are bounded, from forty to ſixty miles diſtance from the ſea-coaſt, with a ridge of mountains, inhabited by ſeveral little bands of rovers, who are

* He has lately been induced to diſpute this point with us.

com-

commanded by chiefs called † Polygars, whom the weakneſs of the government has made inſolent. Theſe robbers plundered the low lands with impunity; by which means the Suba reaped but little benefit from them. Lord Clive firſt recommended them to the attention of the Madraſs preſidency, as neceſſary to command a communication with Bengal. They end, to the northward, about Ganjam, and there the hills fall back a little into the country, winding ſomething from the ſea-coaſt.

The Nizam is governed entirely by his miniſters, and is quite incapable of commanding any of thoſe large tributes which the Suba of the Decan has a right to collect. He is not in the leaſt to be feared, but as he may form junctions with any of the more active powers.

The weſt ſide of the peninſula, diſtinguiſhed by the general name of the Malabar coaſt, extends from Cambay down to Cape Comorine. Along this coaſt, our intercourſe with the natives is very trifling, eſpecially at any diſtance within the land; where we are nearly in the ſame ſituation, as when we firſt ſettled upon that coaſt, excepting that we are now entitled, by the Mogul's grant, to an authority about Surat, which may

† Polygars are the under tributary rajahs.

be turned to very beneficial account under proper management.

As this ſide is but little known, not having hitherto engaged the public attention, I ſhall be fuller, and more particular, in the account I ſhall give of it, becauſe I think it capable of affording very great advantages, in point of revenue, of force, and of trade. The two firſt, independent of the laſt, are now requiſite for the ſecurity of our poſſeſſions on the other ſide, by preſerving the balance of power, and the general tranquillity of the peninſula.

Bombay, which is a ſmall barren iſland, dependent on the continent for ſupport, is the only place we have near Surat, and is our head ſettlement on that ſide : it contains near three hundred thouſand inhabitants. This iſland forms a very fine harbour, with a dock in it fit to receive a ſeventy-four-gun ſhip, and is capable of much improvement. Cloſe adjoining to it lays Salſet, a very fine fertile iſland, and of a large extent. To the northward of Salſet, ſeparated by a ſmall river, lays another large iſland called Baſſeen. They both belong to the Morattahs, as doth the continent for a long extent to the northward and ſouthward of Bombay. Surat is the principal ſettlement to the northward, laying about one hundred and fifty miles from it. The Company have residents, though no settlement, further still to the north, at Scindy and Cambay, which, in a commercial light, are worthy of more attention than has hitherto been paid to them. † Surat has been, for ages, one of the greatest marts in India: it is so commodiously situated for the Gulph of Persia and the Red Sea, that some of the greatest merchants of the East reside there: they are chiefly Moors, with some wealthy Armenians mixed amongst them. What has greatly contributed to increase its wealth and consequence is its being looked upon by the Moors, throughout the empire, as the gate to Mecca.

This part of the country was never properly subdued, until the time of Aurenzeb; as Surat is the place to which all the Moors of India resort in their way to Mecca, it became of great consequence to them; the Mogul therefore established such an authority there, as might secure and protect the pilgrims from any insult or hindrance the Gentoos, who possess most of the country round it, might be tempted to molest them

† Surat lies about twenty miles within the mouth of the river Tappi, which reaches to Brampour, two hundred miles within land, but is not navigable more than ten miles above Surat. The roads from Surat to Cambay are very good, as well as quite into the heart of Indostan, and cross the Decan.

with. The town, and diſtrict belonging to it, was left under the government of a Nabob, or chief magiſtrate, who preſided over the internal police of the inhabitants, and diſtributed juſtice amongſt them in the uſual form; but the Mogul, for greater ſecurity, built a caſtle to command the town, and eſtabliſhed a fleet for the protection of the trade of the port, and to ſcour the coaſt; for the trade along the coaſt, and off the mouth of the river, is often moleſted by roving pirates, who abound in thoſe parts, being tempted to this way of life by the fineneſs of the weather, and the number of convenient retreats along the coaſt. The perſon appointed to the command by the Mogul was both governor of the caſtle and admiral of the fleet. This force was maintained by certain diſtricts near Surat, together with a part of the town and port revenue. At preſent, only a very ſmall part of this revenue is collected for the purpoſes above mentioned, whereof one third only is received by the caſtle, the Nabob of the town has another third, and the remaining third goes to the Morattahs, who alſo hold the greateſt part of the lands that formerly belonged to the caſtle and town. As the empire became rent in pieces by factions, the authority of the governor gradually declined, and the neighbouring princes, no

longer

longer awed by his enfeebled maſter, ſeized on the lands appropriated for the ſupport of the caſtle and fleet, ſince which time, the * Mogul has always given the government to him who could beſt ſupport himſelf in the command. The governor, thus ſtripped of his legal ſupport, plundered the town he was intended to protect, and by this means the trade was almoſt ruined by his oppreſſions.

About the end of 1758, this was the ſtate of Surat, when the preſidency of Bombay, who would no longer endure the oppreſſions and inſults of the † Seiddee, attacked him, deſtroyed his fleet, took the caſtle, and ſettled a treaty with the Nabob.

When the Company had thus got poſſeſſion, the ſhaw (or king) was prevailed on to inveſt them with the title of governor of the caſtle and admiral of the fleet, with the power annexed to it ‡: after that, he left us to ſupport and maintain this grant in the beſt manner we could, for

* Generally confirmed after poſſeſſion, by a grant given, in return for a preſent.

† The Seiddee of Rojapore was then the governor and admiral.

‡ The killa, or caſtle, was allowed a revenue of near 20,000l. a year; 25,000l. a year was allotted for the ſupport of the tanka, or fleet: for the killa, we do not at preſent collect more than 2,500l. a year; nor, for the tanka, more than 4,000l.

the

the lands appropriated for this purpoſe had long been in the hands of the different princes of the country, and the greateſt part of them at preſent belong to Madah-Row, the Morattah prince. Thus we are become the arbiters and the protectors of the town and of its commerce.

The lands formerly belonging to the government of the town and caſtle are now moſtly in the hands of the Morattahs, and yield a revenue of about one hundred and twenty thouſand pounds a-year. The villages and country from whence it is collected lay round about Surat, and extend as low down along the coaſt as Damaun.

As this part of the Malabar coaſt belongs chiefly to the Morattahs, I ſhall here give ſome general deſcription of thoſe people. They conſiſt of ſeveral powerful ſtates, are numerous, rich, and poſſeſs large and fruitful tracts of country. Since the confuſion in the empire, they have ſpread, and much increaſed their power and influence. The Decan, or higher country, together with the Morattah poſſeſſions in Indoſtan, Guzzerat, and the Conkon, with the ſeveral chouts and tributes they demand of the ſtates to the northward and ſouthward of them, are eſtimated all together at ſeventeen crores, or twenty millions four hundred thouſand pounds, a revenue almoſt incredible.

credible. The Nizam, a Moorish prince, is the present Suba of the Decan: a great part of his dominions is contained in this higher country*; his revenue is included in the above twenty millions. Jonojee Bouncello is one of the great Morattah chiefs; his capital is at ‡ Nagpore; he borders on the back of the Bengal provinces; he has about fifty thousand horsemen, that he can assemble under his command. Several other considerable Morattah or Gentoo states are spread about, but laying wide of our connections, we do not know much of them; some of them extend beyond Delhi; the great chief amongst them, by far the most powerful, and whom we are most connected with, is Madah-Row; his dominions reach from Guzarat to Goa; and inland he has, not only the whole of the Conkon, or low country, but a considerable part of the Decan also; the entire revenue belonging to this Morattah state, exclusive of the chouts or tributes from states not under his government, is allowed to be full six millions and a half. Madah-Row is an usurper, and has two competitors,

* The Decan extend from Narmada in the north, to Kama-Sevarah in the south, and yields about twelve crores, or fourteen millions of that great sum.

‡ Nagpore lies about two hundred miles N. E. of Poonah.

petitors, by whom he is kept in a ſtate of anxiety, though they are both confined. The firſt is Ram Rajah, who is the rightful heir and deſcendant of that Rajah of the Decan, who was appointed to this government by Aurenzeb. He was ſeized and impriſoned by Nana, Mada-Row's father, and now remains under bonds at a fort near Settarah. Jonojee Booncello, whom I have mentioned before, is the next heir of Ram Rajah, and ready to put in his claim upon the other's death. The other rival to Mada-Row is his own uncle, Ragoboy, whom he keeps priſoner. Mada-Row is likewiſe obliged, againſt his will, to confine Sudaboy, his father's firſt miniſter and relation, to ſatisfy his preſent miniſters, who helped him to diſpoſſeſs his uncle, and are jealous of Sudaboy's influence and abilities.——I have been more particular in deſcribing the inſecure ſtate of Mada-Row's authority, to ſhew of what advantage to his affairs a connection with the company would prove; and I am ſure his inclination in this reſpect, correſponds with his intereſt. Nor is this alliance leſs profitable to the company. The ſituation and power of Mada-Row being ſuch as enables him to be our moſt valuable friend, or our moſt dangerous enemy. In ſhort the mutual intereſt of both, leads us to each other.

In

In these violent governments, men are so strongly impelled by ambition and fear, that they are easily hurried into rebellion, even when the power of the prince is established, by the justest title to the throne: I think, from what I have here pointed out, it is evident jealousies and animosities might be soon fomented amongst them, should it be found at any time necessary.

Madah-Row, being a bramin, stiles himself only Peshwah or minister, and issues out orders, either from his own authority, or as acting under Ram Rajah, or under the Mogul, as best suits his purposes.—The Morattah country immediately under Madah-Row, the smaller Morattah states, whose princes are tributary to him, and who are obliged to bring a force into the field to join him, whenever he requires them—as I before observed, reach from Guzarat almost to Goa; Gheriah is the southern boundary along the coast, as Hoamso Coat is the inland boundary over to the Carnatic; the Nizam lays on the east side of his dominions, and to the E. from Brampour, large tracts of waste uncultivated lands.—To the northward his dominions extend inland to Chimal in the northern part of Guzarat. Madah-Row, when joined by all his forces, can assemble two hundred thousand horse.—The lands are either under the governors of certain districts and forts, acting immediately under Madah-Row, or under princes who pay him a yearly tribute, and supply him with the troops they are engaged to furnish, whenever he calls upon them. The commanding officers supply their own troops; each body carries with it a buzar (or market) to supply their own quota.—These buzars are often plundered by their own troops, which the officers are obliged to wink at, as they hardly ever pay them for more than half the year. The ammunition is carried by elephants and camels in chests, leather bags, and in duppers, a sort of leathern jars; the chief officers always ride on elephants. Poonah, Madah-Row's capital, lays about one hundred miles inland from Choul, and near fifty beyond the * gotts (or mountains) which separate the lower from the upper country; there are no walls round the city, and it has only horsemen for its defence: Madah-Row has constantly thirty thousand horse attendant on his person.—Within these few years he has been endeavouring to form a body of infantry; but as that method of fighting is very contrary to the genius of

* Gotts are properly passes made over mountains.

the

the people, it will be a long time before they will become of any uſe.—Theſe vaſt bodies of horſe, from the rapidity with which they move, and the devaſtation they leave every where behind them, are only formidable in an enemy's country; their attack is generally made either before the harveſt is gathered in, or whilſt the goods are in the looms; laying waſte with fire and ſword, they ſpread terror and deſolation wherever they go; but cannot long remain in the ſame place, as they depend entirely on plunder for ſupport. Such vaſt armies of horſe, like locuſts, ſoon devour every thing round about them. Tho' if a body of regular troops can once force them to a ſtand, they are preſently diſperſed or deſtroyed.

When Aurenzeb ſubdued this country, and eſtabliſhed a Rajah of the Decan, he gave him power alſo over the ſouthern countries; and it was his buſineſs to exact the chout, or fourth part of their revenues, which they agreed to pay, in order to be exempted from their invaſions; this chout Madah-Row, as acting for the Rajah of the Decan ſtill demands; and ſometimes it is paid him, and ſometimes it is diſputed.

The harbour of Bombay is formed by the continent and ſeveral iſlands, all of which, except Bombay, belong to Madah-

 Row.

Row.—The continent abounds with fine rivers, by which means boats can go a long way up the country, which in the wet ſeaſon are paſſed in boats by the troops, but in the dry many of them are fordable. —From this our ſituation at Bombay, we depend entirely on the Morrattahs for ſupport; this produces a friendly intercourſe of trade between us, as we are furniſhed from his dominions with neceſſaries for our ſubſiſtence, and his ſubjects in return, ſupplied with many of our European commodities.

The Conkon, or low country, extending from Surat quite down to Goa, is bounded inland by one continued ridge of mountains, at the top of which you come into the Decan or higher country, ſo called from your not deſcending again until you get well over to the eaſtward.—Theſe mountains are no where more than fifty miles from the ſea-coaſt, and in ſeveral places within thirty-ſix miles. This ridge of hills forms an almoſt impaſſible barrier to the Conkon from the eaſtward and ſouthward. ——The Morattahs have roads over the hills; but there is not a ſingle paſs, but has been made with much labour and art; and they are ſo defended by forts, either at the ſummit or at the foot of the mountains, that whoever poſſeſſes them cannot

be

be diſlodged without great difficulty.—— Thoſe roads are ſo commodious, that not only *horſe*, *camels*, and *elephants* paſs over, but alſo *carts*, and this without the leaſt hindrance; by which means the Morattahs can open or ſhut the communication as they pleaſe.—In the latitude of Surat the gotts terminate, and loſe themſelves in the level ground; this makes an eaſy paſſage round them; after which, by going to the ſouthward, and croſſing part of the Decan, you reach the Carnatic.

The Morattahs have a revenue from the Conkon of upwards of eight hundred thouſand pounds a-year.—The iſland of Baſſeen yields a revenue to Mada-Row of fifty thouſand pounds—Salſet brings in near ſixty thouſand pounds a-year; Caranjar, a ſmall iſland in the harbour of Bombay, pays eight thouſand yearly; Colaba, a little to the ſouthward of the harbour, eighty-five thouſand a-year; Rajapore, laying about ſixty miles to the ſouthward of Bombay, yields the ſeiddee for his ſmall tract, and two or three forts and an iſland, thirty-ſix thouſand pounds; and the adjacent country ſurrounding the ſeiddee, and extending to the gotts, brings to the Morattahs ninety thouſand pounds yearly.— All this revenue here enumerated, is contained in an extent of country along the ſea

coaſt,

coaſt, not exceeding eighty or ninety miles, and about forty over.

Our marine force on this ſide of India, is ſuperior to all the reſt put together.——The military eſtabliſhment, to judge from the officers, is deſigned to be put upon the ſame footing with the other precedencies; but they are complete only in officers, having but few effective men amongſt the European battalions; and though they are increaſing their ſeipoys, they have not yet near a ſufficient number of battalions of black infantry, to effect any thing upon the continent, or to make ſo large, ſo expenſive an arrangement of high military officers neceſſary.—About four or five years back, the Company had only one major, who commanded the whole military force on that ſide; the engineer, who was alſo the head artillery officer, was a brevet-major—all the reſt were captains.—There is now a general, ſix colonels and lieutenant-colonels, and three majors, beſides a brevet-major to the infantry; the artillery has a lieutenant-colonel and two majors to it—ſhort as the battalions are of their proper number of men, not having more than a third to each company; yet the expence for the military, for the naval, and for the ſervants of the civil departments of Bombay, and its ſeveral ſubordinates, fall very

little

little ſhort of two hundred thouſand pounds a-year, without reckoning any charges for the fortifications, or any extraordinary expences that may ariſe.——Whereas the whole of the revenue ariſing out of the iſland farms, the duties and impoſts of Bombay, and all its dependencies, does not amount to half that ſum a-year.

The gentlemen at Bombay depend entirely on remittances from the other ſettlements, or Europe, to diſcharge the annual balance againſt them, and which muſt at all events be paid, or you riſk the diſbanding, or the mutiny of your troops.——Beſides this, large ſums are expended for fortifications, which have been enlarged, contracted, and enlarged again, and varied and tranſpoſed into different forms, for theſe many years paſt, and will not be, probably, completed for ſome years to come.

All this large expence, together with the annual deficiency for the maintenance of the ſettlement, muſt be paid for by drains from Bengal, or from the profits of the trade of the Malabar coaſt; the whole of which is very inadequate to that purpoſe, becauſe the trade here, for want of money to make the purchaſes, is at ſo low an ebb, that the produce of this coaſt is abſolutely carried off by other nations; and inſtead of having ſeven or eight cargoes from hence, three or four ſhips at moſt are ſent home yearly.

The firſt treaty made with the Morattahs was in governor Law's time, and that treaty ſtill ſubſiſts. The dread of their ſtopping our ſubſiſtence, makes us more ſubſervient to them than is conſiſtent either with our honour or our intereſt, and which ought to be inſeparable.

We might with more eaſe, and as much propriety, aſſume influence on this coaſt, as on the other ſide. This the ſuperiority of our marine would greatly aſſiſt us in obtaining; and many parts of the coaſt, eſpecially to the ſouthward, are in the poſſeſſion of ſmall independent powers, who are conſtantly at variance with each other, and in ſuch a ſtate of anarchy and weakneſs, as would make them eaſily ſubdued, and then formed into what ſyſtem ſhould be thought wiſeſt to eſtabliſh.

Madah-Row has many enemies; and he would wiſh, for various reaſons, to live in friendſhip with us.——A few years ago Ragoboy, his uncle, applied to us for aſſiſtance againſt the Nizam, who had attacked Poonah, and deſtroyed a part of it; he ſtipulated to deliver over to us Salſet, if we would only ſend five or ſix hundred men to his aſſiſtance, and promiſed to put us in possession of the island, as soon as our troops were landed on the continent.—— After repeated solicitations, our governor at last gave him assurance of immediate assistance.—However, an irresolution and delay peculiar to that settlement kept back our troops, by which means we lost our claim; and the Nizam was no sooner informed of our intentions to assist the Morattahs, than he hastened to make peace with them, and returned home.

We have a force capable of molesting the Morattahs very much; the sea-coast we can command, and the divisions between Madah-Row and Hyder might easily be kept up. They are jealous of each other, rivals for power, and of different religions. Yet an inattention to our interest, has made us neglect to improve an intercourse with Madah-Row, and has subjected us to many indignities from his officers.

If that prince had been properly solicited, and every favourable opportunity laid hold of, I doubt not but we might, before this time, have been in the possession of the lands about Surat, which were appropriated by the Mogul for the support of the castle and fleet; we might likewise have been masters of the island of Salset, and such other little spots about the harbour of Bombay, as we should find convenient, without deſtroying the friendly intercourſe between us.

Gheriah is Madah-Row's boundary to the ſouthward; from thence down to Goa the coaſt belongs to the Malwans, and to the * Little Bouncello.—The Malwans join Gheriah to the ſouthward; they are governed by a Rannie or Queen, named Jeezaboy. She is the † widow of Sambojee, a deſcendant of one of the Rajahs ſent down by Aurenzeb to govern this country. I mention this ſo particularly, becauſe a few years paſt we had a war with this queen, and in 1766 poſſeſſed ourſelves of her ‡ fort and country up to the gotts; her revenue is about forty thouſand pounds a-year, and her poſſeſſions reach one hundred miles, or upwards, beyond the mountains, but the whole extent is very narrow.

She agreed to ranſom the fort and country about the coaſt for upwards of ninety thouſand pounds, of this we have received near one half; we have relinquiſhed the place ever ſince 1767, but have not received any of

* So called to diſtinguiſh him from Jonojee Bouncello.

† On which account Madah-Row treats her with ſuch reſpect, as never to be ſeated in her preſence, without her leave; but whenever ſhe dies, as ſhe has only an adopted ſon, Madah-Row will doubtleſs take the country under his care.

‡ Called Sinderdroog.

the remaining part.—The Rannie's capital is called Collipore, and lays about fifty miles beyond the gotts; within five or six miles of her capital, ſhe has a fort called Purnella, where her treaſures are depoſited. —Theſe Malwans who inhabit the ſea-ſide, have always lived by plundering the coaſt, and ſeizing the ſmall veſſels paſſing up and down.

From the Malwans down to Goa the coaſt belongs to the Little Bouncello; his capital is Warree, which is well fortified; it lays about thirty miles inland, and about ten or fifteen miles on this ſide the gotts; at the foot of them he has a ſtrong fort, and along the coaſt he has another, called Raree, not more than twenty or twenty-five miles from Sinderdroog; this fort we took at the ſame time we took Sinderdroog, and the Bouncello agreed to ranſom it for about twenty-five thouſand pounds. On the delivery near half was paid, the remainder is ſtill in arrears. His country reaches ſome miles beyond the gotts, and yields him a revenue of about fifty thouſand pounds a-year.—Goa is in the poſſeſſion of the Portugueze, as was moſt part of the Sounda province (laying at the back of their ſettlement, and to the ſouthward). The Rajah of Sounda has been for ſome time, and is at preſent, a priſoner at Goa, but the Portugueze are ſtripped of the country;

try; of the northern part by Madah-Row, and the ſouthern by Hyder.

* The Bednure kingdom joins to the Sounda province from the ſouthward, and its capital is, from its ſituation, difficult to be attacked; the country, on account of its fertility, is an acquiſition to Hyder of the greateſt conſequence; it abounds with grain, produces great quantities of pepper, beetel-nut, and ſandal, with ſome cardamoms, eſteemed, all of them, moſt excellent in their kind; it affords likewiſe very fine timber for maſts and ſhipping on the ſouthern part, near the port of Mangalore.

The Rajah of this province, who was diſpoſſeſſed by Hyder, is now in the hands of Madah-Row; this country yields a revenue of thirteen or fourteen hundred thouſand pounds.—When Hyder took it, he appointed Yencopoy, a Gentoo of wealth and rank, to the poſt of Duan, or collector of the revenues; and being greatly reduced by his expenſive wars, he has lately ſtripped him of ſome of the † riches he acquired in his former maſter's time.—Mangalore,

* A great many rivers lay along the Malabar Coaſt, many of them will admit of veſſels of conſiderable burthen, and ſome of them are navigable for ſmall ones to within a few miles of the gotts, out of which mountains moſt of theſe rivers ariſe.

† Borrowing of him, a little while ago, 18 lacks of pagodas, or 720,000 l.

the

the moſt conſiderable port Hyder poſſeſſes along the coaſt, lays on the ſouthern boundary of Bednure; it is of the utmoſt importance to him; for by taking it, you ſhut him out from his principal communication with the ſea.—From Mangalore the greateſt part of the produce of the Bednure country is exported, and Hyder has made a convenient road between this port and Siringapatnam, the capital of the Miſour country, where he chiefly reſides.

From Mangalore down to Panani lays that tract of country, once known by the name of the Kingdom of Colaſtria, and which contained the five provinces of *Neleaſaram*, *Cheroka*, *Cotiote*, *Cartenad*, and *Samorine*. Theſe were at that time united under one king, who deputed governors to preſide over the different parts of his dominions.—The Samorines poſſeſs the largeſt of theſe provinces, and *they* firſt revolted. This was many years back; ſince that time the provinces have been governed by ſeparate princes; the prince of Cheroka is the rightful heir of this disjointed kingdom; and the province of Cheroka, the only one that remained to his family on the ſeparation. But even this has lately been conquered from him by Ally Rajah, who reſides in the N. W. part of the province, called Randaterra; the iſland of

Der-

Dermapatam we poſſeſs; and the Cheroka prince, now depending on us for protection and ſupport, reſides in the Braſs Pagoda adjoining to Tellicherry.——Neleaſaram, the northermoſt of theſe five provinces, and adjoining to Bednure, is governed by a prince who is tributary to Hyder. The Cheroka province, which belongs to Ally Rajah, who is a Moor, lays next; he ſtiles himſelf King of the Lucadivæ Iſles, and is a friend and ally of Hyder, under whom he formerly ſerved, and will, in time, no doubt, either for himſelf, or Hyder, extend his conqueſts farther to the ſouthward, if we do not interfere. Ally Rajah is rather inveterate againſt us, for withholding Dermapatam from him.

* The Cotiote province lays next to the Cheroka, on which ſtands Tellicherry, and adjoining to that lays Cartenad, on the N. W. corner of which province ſtands † Mahie.—From thence you enter the Samorines dominion, which produces many valuable articles for trade.—This province is governed by a prince, who is independent, acknowledging no ſuperior, and owing no allegiance.

* The Cotiote and Cartenad provinces have each their ſeparate princes.

† A French ſettlement.

The

The revenues of theſe provinces cannot be eaſily aſcertained, they have ſo often changed maſters, have ſo often been plundered, are engaged in ſuch frequent wars, and are ſo impoveriſhed, that it is impoſſible to form an exact idea of their worth.

The natives of theſe ſouthern countries are in a much more ignorant uncivilized ſtate, than the northern ones.—The Cheroka province can raiſe about twenty thouſand ill diſciplined ſoldiers, and the Samorine can bring into the field about ninety thouſand, ſuch as they are.——It was to march againſt the Bednure Rajah and the Samorines, that Hyder, in 1766, quitted his deſign of attacking the Carnatic. The Bednure, and part of the Sounda countries he conquered, and has kept poſſeſſion of ever ſince; the Samorines and other ſtates he beat and plundered; and he aſſiſted Ally Rajah in ſeizing on the Cheroka province, whilſt its unfortunate prince, who had long been in alliance with us, and the Samorines, with whom we traded, and who aſked for our aſſiſtance, were left to great diſtreſs, we calmly looking on all the while.

From Panani, the ſouthernmoſt boundary of the Samorines dominions, the coaſt down to Cape Comorine belongs to the king of Tra-

Travencore, who lately conquered a conſiderable tract about Cochin *, part of which he holds, and receives tribute from the reſt. He is bounded by the mountains, inland to the eaſt; to the north-eaſt by Madura, belonging to the Carnatic Nabob, and Coimbrature, a province now in Hyder's poſſeſſion; and the Samorines join him to the northward.

The pepper country lays from Goa down to Cape Comorine; and that article is reckoned to increaſe in goodneſs, as you advance to the northward from Anjengo, which lays in the Travencore country, and is the ſouthermoſt ſettlement we have along the coaſt.

Tellicherry is our principal ſettlement to the ſouthward; a great deal of pepper, moſt of the cardamoms, and ſome ſandal are produced in the five provinces round about it. The Company have a reſident at Callicut, in the Samorines dominions, chiefly for the purchaſe of timber.—— They have alſo a reſident at † Onore, for the collection of ſandal and pepper: as this is in the Bednure country, during our

* A Dutch ſettlement.

† A little ſettlement laying within the mouth of a river; ſhips of 200 or 250 tons can paſs the bar at high water, and go into the river; a fortified iſland, ſmall, but high, and difficult of acceſs, commands the entrance of it.

late

late wars with Hyder, we were forced to abandon it.

Having ſhewed how the coaſt from Mangalore to Panani is governed at preſent, it is very evident, that theſe little ſtates, on account of their diviſions and their want of diſcipline, muſt fall a prey to Hyder, whenever he chuſes to invade them again, or to ſupport Ally Rajah againſt them; unleſs we protect them.

Since therefore they are not likely to remain long with their preſent poſſeſſors, the point in queſtion ſeems to be, in my opinion, whether, by protection, and a proper aſcendency over them, we ſhall lead them to civilization, and teach them, by induſtry, to obtain the comforts and conveniencies of life, enriching at the ſame time, both themſelves and us? Or, whether Hyder, by conqueſt, ſhall force them into ſlavery, and, by increaſing his ſtrength, oblige us to forſake our ſettlements?—For it is at the back of theſe five provinces the Miſour country lays, which Hyder Ally uſurped from its lawful prince, who is a Gentoo, as were all the natives, until Hyder brought Moors amongſt them.—He has conquered Coimbature, adjoining to the Miſour from the ſouthward, and he has alſo added the Bednure, and part of the Sounda countries to his dominions. This is all the ſea-coaſt he can command, except what is under Ally Rajah, who, I doubt not, might eaſily be drawn from his alliance. Hyder's capital Seringapatnam lays about one hundred and fifty miles inland from Mangalore, from which ſide only Hyder is vulnerable.

The Miſour country is very extenſive; it reaches over to the Carnatic, and is bounded to the ſouthward by Madura, to the weſtward lay the five provinces which ſeparate it from the Malabar Coaſt, to the northward it is joined by the Bednure country, and to the N. E. of it lays the Decan, where Hyder alſo has made ſome encroachments *.

The king of Travencore may make ſome ſmall ſtand againſt Hyder, ſhould he ever attack him; but without our aſſiſtance, he would ſoon be overpowered.

I have now taken a general view of the Malabar Coaſt, and Hyder's dominions; and I have endeavoured to ſhew how the two moſt powerful ſtates of the peninſula, and the moſt likely to diſturb it, are ſituated.

If we purſue our real intereſt, we ſhall endeavour to form an alliance with the Morattahs, as the moſt powerful aſſiſtants againſt the attempts of Hyder, who is our

* He now poſſeſſes the ſtrong fort of Bengalure.

dan-

dangerous enemy; and ſo he muſt always continue, becauſe he knows it is our intereſt to reduce him.

If he ſhould ever get poſſeſſion of the Carnatic, we ſhould lay at his mercy for all our inveſtments along the Coromandel Coaſt; and if in ſuch a caſe he ſhould be able to overpower, as it is moſt likely he would, the little ſtates that lye round about him, we ſhould equally depend upon his pleaſure, for all the produce of the Malabar Coaſt, from Goa downwards.— The port of Mangalore, and his connection with Ally Rajah, afford him an opportunity of calling in a body of French troops, and of eaſily conveying them into the Miſour country, and he has it in his power to reward them.

In order to prevent this misfortune, it would be right policy to re-eſtabliſh the lawful Rajahs of Bednure and Sounda: this would be an act of great juſtice, as well as prudence, and might be the means of obtaining the port of Mangalore; and ſecuring the trade of the province.——It would beſides be a very ſevere blow to Hyder, and ſhut him out from all intercourſe with the ſea-coaſt.

His repeated inſolent behaviour to us, ought to rouſe us from our lethargy, for it is by vigor only that we can aſſure quiet to the Carnatic.

I think it evident from what I have ſaid, that the Company ought to turn their eyes to the Malabar Coaſt, and endeavour to obtain more territory on that ſide, not only for the maintainance of their ſettlements, and the increaſe of their trade in thoſe parts, but likewiſe for the ſecurity of their poſſeſſions on the eaſt ſide of the peninſula, which cannot be firmly eſtabliſhed without an intercourſe of power between the two coaſts.—Not that I mean to recommend extenſive conqueſts, or wide acceſſion of dominion. My aim is confined to a few objects, which might be eaſily obtained by treaty, and would, upon proper conſiderations, be given up to us almoſt as ſoon as propoſed. Such are firſt the lands formerly allotted for the ſupport of the caſtle and fleet at Surat, which are our undoubted right, as we are inveſted with the government of that fort for the Mogul; next the iſlands of Baſeen, Salſet, and Caronjar*. Beſides this the bay of Carwar, and the port of Mangalore, together with the entrance of ſome of the ſouthern rivers.

* Caronjar commands the entrance of Penn River.

It will not be foreign to the present subject, to give a sketch of Hyder's conduct for some years past, that the public may see how necessary it is to have an eye upon his ambition, and to adopt some resolute system to check his growing power, and to withstand his encroachments. Our conduct hitherto has been so timid in this respect, to say no worse, that we gained no honour in the war, and lost much reputation in the peace, which is not only disgraceful, but precarious.

Hyder is bold and ambitious: he is a good soldier, and an able statesmen; and was trained up in the European service. About the middle of 1766, it was discovered he was making an alliance with the Nizam, to invade the Carnatic; and was actually advancing for that purpose, when those troubles on the Malabar coast, already mentioned, called him back; being embroiled with the Bednure Rajah, (whose country he had seized,) and with the Samorines and other small states, some of which he took, and some he plundered *.

* Ally Rajah invited him down to plunder the Samorines, &c. tempting him by the prospect of gain. On finding himself disappointed, he threatened Ally Rajah with death, if he did not procure him money.—Ally Rajah, by good fortune, took two boats coming out of the Samorine dominions, loaded with pagodahs, to deposit with some of the Europeans, and by that means saved his head.

This

This was the favourable moment to have attacked Hyder, and we ought to have availed ourſelves of it; for if at that time we had bent our views againſt Mangalore and Seringapatnam, and part of the forces from Madraſs had been ſent round to the Malabar coaſt, to be joined to thoſe from Bombay, they might, in ſix days from their landing at Mangalore, have been at Hyder's capital. And, as to the Nizam, the leaſt ſhadow of a force would have brought him to terms, if Hyder could have been employed elſewhere, by any diverſion.—The knowledge of Hyder's character ſhould have taught our governors, that force, and force only, could put a ſtop to his ambitious purſuits; but, unfortunately, the politics of India at this time were of another caſt, and the plan was to temporize, negotiate, and protract.

We continued in this inactive ſtate at Madraſs until the middle of 1767, when we found Hyder, after quieting every thing round about him, was preparing to join the Nizam, and advance again to the Carnatic. War was then inevitable; and ſuch was the conſequence of protracting the evil day, that we thereby enabled the enemy to chuſe his own time, and to give us the deeper wound.

In

In the beginning of 1768, a force from Bombay took Mangalore from Hyder; but it was no ſooner taken, than it was in effect abandoned; and yet Hyder thought the loſs of this place of ſuch conſequence, that, upon receiving the intelligence, he immediately marched back from * Bengalore, in order to recover it, though at that very time the Madraſs army was marching to attack that important fort.

The Nizam's troops were ſoon diſperſed by general Smith; but Hyder returned as ſoon as Mangalore was retaken, and penetrated into the Carnatic.

The true way of attacking Hyder's dominions was to have carried the war to the weſt ſide of the peninſula, where the way was open, and we could have marched into the heart of his country, and laid ſiege to his capital in a few days from Mangalore. Inſtead of that we choſe to attack him from the eaſt, which was impracticable.—This capital error produced fatiguing marches, and very great expences; the general was ſubjected to the controul of field-deputies, and theſe deputies, I do not affirm it, but I have been credibly ſo informed, were alſo the contractors for the army.—Complaints aroſe of the want of proper ſupplies; the general found

* Is a frontier garriſon of Hyder's, laying on the confines of the Decan, and near the Carnatic.

him-

himſelf unable to penetrate into Hyder's country, thro' ſuch tracts of waſte and woody lands, and over ſuch deep rivers as he had to paſs. During all this time it was almoſt impoſſible to bring our enemies to an action, who, with their numerous horſe, were ſpoiling the country; the manufactures were deſtroyed, and the Carnatic laid waſte; while an immenſe ſum, not leſs than five or ſix hundred thouſand pounds, was drawn from Bengal to defray the charges of this war; ſo greatly did it exceed the revenues of Madras. And yet Hyder, after doing all this miſchief, found himſelf as far from conquering the Carnatic, as when he firſt began; his ſtrength greatly exhauſted; and the remains of his army brought to ſuch a ſituation by our general, that he could not retreat without fighting; for the Nizam did nothing*.—Under theſe difficulties, Hyder, who knew the temper of our gentlemen, whoſe public as well as private intereſt depended on the fate of the Carnatic, had the art to work upon their fears, and prevailed upon them to ſtop the motions of the army, to give him a paſſport to the walls of Madraſs; and at laſt to accede to a treaty very

* After being defeated in one or two battles, he made peace and went home.

inconſiſtent with our intereſt, and even our honour; this treaty was ſigned the 3d April, 1769.—And tho' the three great preſidencies are independent of each other, nevertheleſs the gentlemen of Madraſs, without ever properly conſulting the governor and council of Bombay, whoſe intereſts and connections they were but ſlightly acquainted with, and over whom they have not the leaſt ſhadow of authority, ſtipulated for them equally with themſelves; to aſſiſt Hyder in caſe he was attacked, without enquiring into the juſtice of his quarrel, tho' by ſuch a blind compliance, we were liable to be continually involved in diſputes.—We alſo ſuffered Hyder to take away from under our protection at Madraſs, the remains of Chanda Saib's family *; Mahomed Ally's inveterate enemy; and whom he now has ready to ſet up as a rival to the preſent Nabob of the Carnatic, whenever he ſees proper. The Carnatic is now beginning to recover itſelf †, but as likely as ever to be invaded and laid waſte by Hyder, whenever he is at leiſure, and chuſes again to attack it.

* Hyder has lately married his ſon to one of the family.

† For by the great care of our governor on that coaſt, the trade of the Carnatic was, about the year 1766, that is, before the war, brought to a more flouriſhing ſtate than it had been in for many years back.

Hyder had no ſooner extricated himſelf from his danger, by means of the peace he made under the walls of Madraſs, than a quarrel enſued between him and the Morattahs.—Madah-Row having demanded the chout, or fourth part of the revenues *, the Miſour and Bednure countries uſed to pay him, together with the poſſeſſion of the fortreſs of Bengalore.

Hyder has been repulſed with loſs, in one or two engagements with the Morattahs, who are at preſent rather an overmatch for him, and will continue ſo, unleſs called off by ſome northern invaſions.—Hyder, to prevent the gentlemen of Bombay from forming any alliance with Madah-Row, who had made ſome overtures for that purpoſe, ſent a vackeel (or envoy) to the preſidency, about the end of 1769, to deſire ſome man of rank and underſtanding might be ſent with full powers to ſettle with him, agreeable to the terms of the Madraſs treaty, and to adjuſt every thing relative to our commerce with his country, promiſing to deliver up ſome priſoners who fell into his hands, on the retaking Mangalore and Onore in May 1768, and who had from that time been in confinement.

* Upwards of 30 lack.

The governor, inſtead of ſending a memberof the board, ſent only two junior ſervants, to whom no full powers could be given.—Hyder releaſed the priſoners, but treated the two gentlemen with indignity, making them follow him from place to place, until he reached his capital, and then made them wait ſeveral days in the ſuburbs, before he would ſee them.

Hyder, about the middle of the year 1770, ſigned a treaty with the governour of Bombay; induced to it merely by the hopes of preventing us from engaging with the Morattahs; for he ſtill continues much diſguſted with us, and thinks the Madraſs treaty not adhered to.—The Morattahs, on the other ſide, think themſelves ſlighted, and aſcribe our alliance with Hyder to fear: ſo that we are upon the worſt terms with both.—And while we are aggrandizing Hyder, who it is impoſſible can ever cordially unite with us, we are riſking the reſentment of the Morattahs, who would have been our good allies, if we had properly purſued our own intereſt.

PART III.

Measures to be pursued.

I Have given this view of the powers, states, and kingdoms upon the coast of Malabar, to shew how intimately the politics of one coast are connected with the other; and how necessary it is to enlarge our plan upon the western side of the peninsula; and I have endeavoured to point out the mistakes and irregularities that have been committed in our several presidencies, from the false policy of the rulers, in adhering to the old system of government; and from the too great desire of gain in individuals; this I have done, hoping that the parliament may be induced to take this important subject into their consideration before it is too late.

It is on the increase of all the different manufactures and growths of the two * *coasts*, and at Bengal, and on their prices, that all our advantages ultimately depend. These can only be secured by preventing the money from being sent out of the country; by placing commerce on such an equality, that the ballance shall incline only in favour of

* Coromandel and Malabar.

industry;

induſtry; and by placing property in a ſtate of ſafety ſo ſecure, that the ſtrong cannot force it from the weak.—No policy can be more uſeful, than to impreſs upon the minds of the natives the ſtrongeſt aſſurance of freedom and ſecurity under our laws.—The trade being increaſed by theſe means, will draw after it, of courſe, an increaſe of wealth and population.—Our provinces will ſwarm with inhabitants; the induſtrious will flock there for employment, the opulent for ſhelter, and the whole riches of Indoſtan will finally center in our dominions.—Some ſpeedy regulations muſt be inforced, to prevent that ſudden, and till lately unheard-of, means of acquiring fortunes: gentlemen thereby imbibe a contempt for trade, the very end for which they are ſent out; luxury and indolence have got too much footing in all the preſidencies, and too general a neglect and inattention prevails.—Young men, with ſcarcely any more knowledge than they brought with them, after a few years reſidence, are advanced to important poſts, where they are obliged, as unforeſeen accidents ariſe, and intricate circumſtances preſent themſelves, to form opinions, and manage affairs of the greateſt conſequence, without judgment or experience to direct them.—Theſe youths are not ſo blameable as thoſe who ſend them forth, without eſtabliſhing regulations for their conduct,

conduct, which ſhould on no account be diſpenſed with.

It is from this omiſſion that they ſo ſoon forget the end for which they engaged; and that they run into ſuch exceſſes of extravagance and diſſipation, as render the brighteſt capacities unfit for buſineſs, and frequently occaſion real loſs to their country.

The number of civil ſervants far exceeds the demand, in all the three preſidencies. The free merchants and mariners are increaſed beyond what can poſſibly be provided for in the commerce either by ſea or land. I do not ſee how one third part of them can be employed, were they ever ſo induſtrious; but the want of occupation, and the habits of thoſe eaſtern climates render men unfit for labour. The only alternative remaining for the real intereſt of the Company is either to colonize, or to reduce the number.

The trade to the different parts of India, carried on by the Company's ſervants and private merchants, is greatly overdone, I mean here the foreign, as diſtinguiſhed from the inland trade; if we except the freight-ſhips to the gulphs, there is ſcarcely a voyage ſet on foot that does not prove a loſing one: moſt of the gentlemen trade beyond what their capitals will bear, and intereſt is there remarkably high, a proof the medium, by which the trade is carried on, is far ſhort of the neceſſary demand.

At

At Madrass, indeed, the principal trade of late years has been with the Nabob, by lending him money at a high interest on his bond, by which means a very large property has been locked up, which would otherwise have circulated about India for the general benefit of trade.

Harmony ought carefully to be kept up between the gentlemen intrusted with the civil power, and those who command the military: the army ever must be under the controul of the civil power, except as to its manœuvre and arrangements, and in the course of execution: these particulars should be entirely under the direction of the superior military officer; for it is absurd in a civil governor to interfere in every little regulation, and in points it is morally impossible he can ever be properly acquainted with: why he should wish it, I know not, since, by meddling on every such occasion, he adds nothing to his own consequence, but diminishes that of the commander in chief of the troops, and gives general disgust: jealousy prevails too often between these two different departments, and is productive of feuds, that may at some time or other prove fatal to the general interest of the Company.

Most of the eastern princes near us have artful spies in their pay, to inform them of the

the tempers and underſtandings of thoſe gentlemen who preſide over the preſidencies and their ſubordinate ſetttlements. And it has often happened, that reſolutions which ſhould have been kept ſecret, have tranſpired before they have been carried into execution. Henceit is, the princes offer to inſult us, or prudently deſiſt, according to the diſpoſition they diſcover in us to reſent or overlook any improper behaviour.

Though there are extraordinary inſtances of courage in individuals, yet puſillanimity is the predominant characteriſtic of the Indian ſtates, and therefore they ſupply the want of courage by treachery.—Lord Clive ſoon diſcovered this, and took advantage of it, by ſhewing great firmneſs and reſolution on all occaſions, tempering them with the ſtricteſt juſtice.

The rulers at home, from whom all the great appointments flow, and under whoſe direction the general ſyſtem is to be conducted, have not ſuch thorough information from abroad as their ſituation requires, wherein their own ſervants have been too negligent and remiſs, they ought long before this time to have given the directors a complete knowledge of the ſtrength, the revenues, and the produce of the ſeveral countries in the peninſula; their internal advantages, the forms of government, and the diſpoſition of the natives, their ſeveral

intereſts

interests and connections with each other, their different dependencies, the abilities of their princes, the avenues to their countries, whether from the land or sea, where most defencible, and from whence easiest to be attacked.

It might be better upon the whole, as I have before observed, if we could return back to our commercial system; but that is impossible. Ignorance kept us in a state of confinement, ambition knew not then how to act; knowledge led us to the means, and various accidents have placed us in our present situation. That insatiate desire after wealth and power, which possesses every civilized nation, will not allow us to retreat; we must preserve our consequence, or be trampled under foot.

The government of the rich and extensive possessions we have gained, demand abilities greatly superior to those, which might suffice for the management of our commerce, whilst it stood unconnected with the political system, for at present it is on our political conduct that our trade here wholly depends.

If any one will take a review of human nature, and consider how much we are under the influence of our passions, how apt the best of us are to be hurried by them into excesses, how in one situation, the ſame thing may be reconciled to our inward ſeelings, which, in another ſituation, would ſtrike us with a conſcious meanneſs to attempt. If he will reflect how difficult it is to reſiſt ſuch large emoluments, which, without ſeeking, fall in our way, and which, if one man refuſes, we know another will take up; and that theſe evils do not ariſe ſo much from our miſconduct, as the faſhion of the conſtitution, and the imperfections of a miſerable ſyſtem of government, eſtabliſhed in the countries conqueſt made us maſters of, and which no proper care has ever been taken to ſearch into and amend—If any one, I ſay, will enter into theſe conſiderations, he will ſee at once how neceſſary, and at the ſame time how impoſſible it is to reform any of theſe flagrant abuſes by the feeble authority of the directors, who have no controul over thoſe ſervants, that they are obliged to intruſt with powers almoſt deſpotic.—It is the controul of laws over the rulers, that conſtitutes the ſole difference betwixt the ſtate of tyranny and freedom. This ſhews the abſurdity of ſupervisors; for they were, in fact, inveſted with much higher power, than any one preſidency enjoyed over the country under its juriſdiction;—and what, in the name of God, is there in the title of Supervisor, to exempt a man from temptation,

tion, more than in the title of Governour. I have not the leaſt reſentment againſt any individual; I envy no man his ſucceſs; long may they proſper, and enjoy their fortunes; but I feel for the Company, for I have long ſeen them verging towards ruin; and I now ſee them, in my own opinion, haſtening to an end. In ſuch a ſituation we cannot be too open, nothing ſhould lay hid; I am ſatisfied the beſt chance the Company and the nation (for the concern is too great to ſeparate them) have of avoiding the impending blow, is by a fair and open ſtate of their real condition.—— With which view, I will endeavour to ſhew the public my idea of their danger, and the fatal conſequence of the cruſh I am apprehenſive of.

The great fund upon which the Company has hitherto depended to reduce their accumulated debts, and anſwer the great increaſe of their expences to government and to themſelves, was the overflowing of the Bengal revenue; this revenue has been annually decreaſing to that degree, that inſtead of affording any ſupply to China, the gentlemen abroad have been obliged this laſt year, to draw upon the Company for part of the inveſtments of Bengal.—This being the caſe, the Company have nothing at home, but their profits, to pay their debts, and to defray their expences. We will allow the famine has bore hard upon Bengal the last year, and that another year the settlement will be better off; yet, in the declining state of that country, the revenues are not likely, without a total change of system, to recover their proper state; and should a change take place, the effect will require some time to shew itself.——If therefore (which may soon be the consequence) their debts abroad should increase, and their cargoes, for want of money to purchase, fall short; or if the remittances, by bills, should exceed their abilities to pay, and no collateral security be in the directors hands to induce the Bank to lend, the Company are then undone. *

If this was to happen, the gentlemen who have lent their money towards the Company's investments in India, would immediately have recourse to the Company's effects there, for the recovery of their debts; this would prevent our receiving any assistance from that quarter; and the revenues, which have hitherto been the great support of all, would be sunk in anarchy and confusion: no money to advance to the Aurungs, consequently no cargoes; and the troops ill paid, would increase the disorder, by stimulating each other to seek

new

new maſters, or to join in plundering the country; nor would their officers be able to reſtrain them.

Thus would Bengal fall into a moſt diſtracted ſtate, and be left to ſettle itſelf, in what manner chance ſhould determine. Our own private merchants, who are liable to forfeit their goods, if they bring them round the Cape, could only trade to the Gulphs. Therefore all the goods brought to Europe, would center with the foreign companies.

It is the ſurplus of this great revenue that has enabled the Company to make the figure they have done of late years. This it is that has made good the inveſtments in India.—This has ſupplied Madraſs, Bombay, and China, by which means, as they had no occaſion to return much of their capital to India, the amount of their ſales at home, has been great part of it applied to anſwer all the various demands upon them, and to increaſe their dividend.

This is the ſtate of Bengal. As to Madraſs, that ſettlement, I do admit, would ſupport itſelf, if it remained undiſturbed, and alſo yield a conſiderable annual gain to Leadenhall-Street; but this is only to be done in its moſt flouriſhing ſituation.

Bombay,

Bombay, in its preſent ſtate, is a true picture of poverty and pride; it makes a ſplendid appearance, with nothing to ſupport it—not all the profits of its trade, joined to its revenues, being equal to the expences: it is a burthen, rather than any real advantage, as it now ſtands. Therefore, if Bengal fails ſending ſupplies to Bombay, that ſettlement muſt be left to ſcramble for itſelf.

And as to the trade of China, where we have no credit, if we can ſend but little money, and few goods, that would ſoon vaniſh and be annihilated.—The immediate loſs to the government here, would be felt in the deficiencies of the cuſtoms and exciſe, to ſay nothing of the four hundred thouſand pounds a-year, ſettled at the laſt agreement.—At the ſame time that other nations, by bringing home the trade, would draw away our money to ſupply us with the luxuries of life.

If to this account we add, what would neceſſarily enſue, the great reduction of ſhips now annually employed, the different manufactures of this kingdom they require to fit them out, the wages they pay for labour, the ſeamen they train up, and the different goods produced in this kingdom, which the private adventurers, ſervants of the Company, leave behind in

India;

India; the loſs to the nation could never be deſcribed or conceived, until it was felt; ſuch a loſs would be a long time, if ever, before it could be recovered.

Commerce is of that intricate nature, that, like the overflowing of the Nile, we are ſenſible of its effect, without being able to trace it to its ſource. We all know that credit and riches are neceſſary for its ſupport; we alſo know that it flouriſhes moſt, when aſſiſted by induſtry and œconomy. We perceive it gathering and increaſing, but by ſuch imperceptible ways, as are never to be clearly found out; and we know, when once it has changed its courſe, it is ſeldom brought back again.

Gentlemen may ſay that the picture I have drawn is more in imagination than in reality, or at leaſt the evil day is far off: I wiſh it may be ſo.—I will allow it may be warded off for a few years, but it will prove fatal from a lingering delay, whereas by timely aſſiſtance, I am ſatisfied they may become more flouriſhing than ever, at leaſt it is worth attempting.—For who in a decline, however ſure of wearing out a length of years, would not run ſome hazard for the chance of perfect health.

This, however, I am ſure of, conteſts and animoſities, raiſed by jealouſy and reſentment, have frequently diſtracted the

councils

councils at home and abroad; party has had too great a ſhare in determining points of moment—and political miſtakes have, at times, done great injury to different branches of our commerce.——What has been adopted by one ſet of men, the next has often diſapproved; the leaders, under every change, oppoſed, attacked, and delayed in their purſuits, governing diſtant ſtates, without the power of either puniſhment or retroſpection, ſurrounded with difficulties, and frequently wandering in a maze of error; all this, if it continues, will, and muſt, in a few years, involve our public credit, together with the Company, in one general ruin.

The preſent ſtate of the Eaſt India Company's affairs, calls loudly for reformation; and its complicated extenſive views, are an object of great national conſequence. If parliament does not take it under conſideration, it is irretrievably gone—the fair and honeſt ſtock-holder [for I mean to ſeparate him from the jobber in the Alley] will be almoſt ruined; the bondholders may probably be ſaved, but government will greatly ſuffer—the crown revenues from the India Company will be hardly worth collecting, and one great vend for the manufactures of this country will be ſtopped;—for the trade can never be carried on, but by a company, inveſted with an exclusive right; nor can the government ſecure their duties by any other method.

The authority unavoidably inveſted in the gentlemen who take the lead abroad, calls for great abilities to execute, and the ſovereign power to controul.—No part of the executive power ſhould ever be in a ſituation to over-rule, or counteract with impunity, that power on which it depends; this has ſometimes been the caſe in India. —It is not poſſible for the directors to apply the remedy; the ableſt men this nation can produce, as directors, never can effect it. It is from the wiſdom of parliament only the plan muſt be formed, and the ſyſtem to be purſued marked out.—It is, in my opinion, an object well worthy their attention; and it can only be carried into execution, and maintained by the immediate authority of the ſovereign.

Thus have I endeavoured to point out the advantages that would reſult to theſe kingdoms, from a diſintereſted and well conducted government in India; wherein I have been under a neceſſity of laying open the errors and miſconduct of many perſons towards whom I do not bear the leaſt reſentment or animoſity. I would rather wiſh to draw a veil over all that is paſt; for I am convinced, mankind oftener err through falſe miſtaken judgments, than from a want of principle; therefore retroſpects, in general, I abhor.——Remove the evil, all will be well; the Company will again flouriſh, and permanency be given to their commerce.

Change the men as often as you pleaſe; call them governours or ſupervisors, for the difference is only in the name; yet, if the ſame maxims of government remain, if the ſame temptations, with the ſame impunity, fall in their way, mankind will, upon the whole, be found every where alike: it is circumſtances and ſituation only, that make the apparent difference.

The facts I have here laid down, I know to be true. The opinions and ideas are my own, perhaps erroneous; but ſuch as they are, they have been formed in my cooleſt hours of reflection, and will remain fixed and unaltered, till my ſentiments arech nged by conviction, which I am as ready to receive, as any perſon can be, who has no intereſt of his own in view.

I have attempted to ſhew the principal impediments in the way of the nation's reaping a laſting benefit from the trade to the Eaſt Indies. But the regulations, by which the political and military powers ſhall be ſeparated from the commercial one, giving to the Company ſuch freedom and independency, as ſhall ſecure it from all impediments, will require the matureſt conſideration.

It muſt be left to thoſe who are better acquainted with human nature, who know the proper limitations to be given to power, and how to make the various ſprings and movements, dependent on each other, co-operate together; and who know how to ſet ſo complicated a ſyſtem in motion, and to keep it ſo.

F I N I S.

ERRATUM.

Page 47, in the note, *for* Kama-Sevarah *read* Rama-Sevarah.

www.ingramcontent.com/pod-product-compliance
Lightning Source LLC
Chambersburg PA
CBHW032245080426
42735CB00008B/1015
* 9 7 8 3 3 3 7 0 5 9 3 7 8 *